MOVE

**From Despondency to Destiny
Your Destiny awaits!**

STUDY GUIDE

Frizella Taylor

TaylorMade Publishing

www.TaylorMadePublishingFL.com
904-323-1334

Unless otherwise indicated, all scripture references are from King James Version (KJV)

The Amplified Bible (AMP)

New Living Translation (NLT)

New International Version (NIV)

The Message (MSG)

The Passion Translation (TPT)

MOVE

From Despondency to Destiny Study Guide

ISBN: 978-0-9968123-7-5, copyright © 2020

Cover Photo Paul Smith on Unsplash

FRIZELLA TAYLOR

Jacksonville, FL, USA

All rights reserved under International copyright law. Contents and or cover may not be reproduced in whole or part in any form without the express written consent of the publisher.

For additional copies, please visit our website:

www.frizelladonegantaylor.com

www.taylormadepublishingfl.com

Table of Contents

Introduction i
How to Use This Study Guide ii
   Welcome to this study guide! ii
Prayer of Salvation 1
Lesson 1: What is the Issue? 2
   Non-Marital Relationships 2
   Marriage 3
   Divorce 4
   Death of a Loved One 5
   Persecution by Others 5
Lesson 2: How to Understand Divine Appointment 8
   Encounters of a Divine Appointment 9
   Joshua, Moses is Dead 9
   Saul / Paul 9
Lesson 3: How Does God Guide Me? 13
   My Guiding Journey 13
   God Guides by His Word 14
Lesson 4: How Do I Follow the Voice of God? 17
   An Example of Hearing God Through His Word 17
   You Must Understand God's Voice 19
Lesson 5: Arriving in Destiny! 21
   On the Road to Destiny! 21
   You Have Arrived at Destiny! 22
Lesson 6: How to Stay on Destiny's Track 25
   How Does Prayer Keep You on Track? 25
   How Does Wise Council Keep You on Track? 27
   How Do Strategic Plans Keep You on Track? 28
   How Does Perseverance Keep You on Track? 29
Lesson 7: Healing in the Emotions 32
   Your Emotions Can Be Healed! 33

   God's Plan for Healing You 34
   What will it Take? FAITH? 35
Your One Page Strategic Plan 38
Conclusion 41
About the Author 42
About the Publisher 43
Books by Frizella 44

Introduction

As you move through life, you find that situations, issues failures, and successes are inevitable. "Life happens." Some things are good, and some things are bad. Regardless of which situation you are in today, do not allow it to stop you from pursuing God and the things that He has for you to do.

These situations and circumstances will get in the way of your progress and prevent you from moving forward. When this happens, you must figure out how to move beyond your past so you can move into your destiny. Your destiny is connected to a divine appointment as ordered by the Lord. Therefore, maneuvering through life becomes a timely manner. It all depends on the Lord's timing and your willingness to follow the path He puts before you.

In this study guide, we will look at, discuss, and discover what "Move, From Despondency to Destiny, Your Destiny Awaits" means. What is it? How do you recognize it? How do you respond to it? Moreover, why should you respond to it? "It" is your past, your destiny. Then, we will look at ways in which God can guide you into your destiny using divine appointments. Further, we will learn how to know that God is leading us and how to avoid missing HIM.

Lastly, we will learn and understand how to hear God's voice and follow His leading. With this in mind, you will be able to walk into your destiny and not allow life's pressure to deter you.

How to Use This Study Guide

Welcome to this study guide!

This course of study is designed to help you discover your calling. It is beneficial in catapulting your spiritual development and to aid you to walk into your destiny. This guide is useful for individual or group study.

To be successful, make a personal commitment to allow time to do each lesson/question to the best of your ability. Be honest with yourself when identifying issues. Be intentional about your personal growth and healing process to become the best YOU. As you proceed through this guide, ask the Holy Spirit to show you your heart, your issue(s) and how to overcome them.

Additional guidelines to be successful:

1. Start each lesson with prayer. Ask the Holy Spirit, for wisdom, clarity and understanding.
2. Pace yourself to get the full benefit of each lesson by not moving too quickly through the material.
3. When possible, use a physical Bible and mark each scripture reference.
4. Make personal notes when the Holy Spirit speaks to you.
5. Answer all applicable questions, remember there are no right or wrong answers, be honest.
6. Be committed to MOVE forward in the LORD for you own sake.

Prayer of Salvation

Scripture references: John 3:1-7; 13-17; Romans 6:23, 10:8-13

If you want your prayers answered you must have a personal relationship with the Son, Jesus Christ. The Bible tells us, in John 14:57 that Jesus is the way to the Father; "Thomas said to him, "Lord, we don't know where you are going, so how can we know the way? Jesus answered, "I am the way and the truth and the life. No one comes to the Father except through Me. If you really know Me, you will know My Father as well. From now on, you do know Him and have seen Him." Pray this prayer:

Dear Heavenly Father, I come to You in the name of Jesus, and I confess that Jesus is Lord, I believe that He died on the cross for my sins and rose on the third day by the power of God and is now seated on the right hand of the heavenly Father continually making intercession on my behalf.

You said if I call upon the name of Jesus I would be saved. I am calling on Jesus name now, I know that I am a sinner; I realize that I cannot make it on my own. I ask you to forgive me of all my sins.

I ask that Jesus would come into my life and give me the power to live for Him. Father, thank You for Your Word, thank You for sending Your son Jesus to this world to die for my sins, sickness, and disease. I ask that Your, kingdom will come into my life that I may receive the free gift of eternal life.

Satan, I serve you notice that you have no more power over my life. I am now a child of the most-high God. I rebuke you Satan, and the blood of Jesus is against you! I denounce every foul thing that you have sent my way and in the name of Jesus, I command you to go!! In Jesus Name AMEN!

Lesson 1: What is the Issue?

This lesson will assist you in discovering any issues that may be holding you back. Work through the questions thoroughly and be honest with yourself as this will allow your healing to manifest.

Q.1a List three major things that prevent you from moving forward or slow you down?

1. _____
2. _____
3. _____

Q.1b Share a scenario where you recognized one of the issues above:

_____
_____
_____

Q.1c Once you discovered the issue, what steps did you take to rectify the issue?

_____
_____
_____

Q.1d In chapter 1, page 2 in the book, it lists some common issues that can stand in the way of your destiny. Can you identify other areas that have become stumbling blocks in you moving forward?

_____
_____
_____

Non-Marital Relationships

Q.1e Describe a situation where you and a friend or co-worker had a disagreement and stopped speaking:

_____
_____
_____

Q.1f   Were you able to come back from the fall out?

_____
_____
_____

Q.1g   How has that relationship disagreement affected you?

_____
_____
_____

Marriage

Q.1h   List three things from your marital problems that you feel have affected your moving forward?

1. _____
2. _____
3. _____

Q.1i   How have these issues you listed affected you?

_____
_____
_____

Q.1j   How have the issues you listed affected your children or other family members?

_____
_____
_____

Q.1k   How have you dealt with these issues?

_____
_____
_____

Divorce

Q.1l On page 5 of the book, there is a list of emotions associated with divorce. Do you identify with any? If so how?

_____
_____
_____

Q.1m Are there any other emotions you have dealt with from your divorce?

_____
_____
_____

Q.1n How has the divorce altered the way you live?

_____
_____
_____

Q.1o Do you feel you have been healed from your divorce?

_____
_____
_____

Q.1p Have you found your "place" since being divorced?

_____
_____
_____

Q.1q How has being happily married hindered you from fulfilling your destiny?

_____
_____
_____

Q.1r How have you involved your spouse in your destiny?

Death of a Loved One

Q.1s Has the death of a loved one altered your life? If so, how?

Q.1t How have you handled the grief associated with the death of your loved one?

Q.1u Do you feel you have moved past the pain associated with the death of your loved one?

Persecution by Others

Q.1v Describe how you felt when someone deliberately persecuted you:

Q.1w How did you overcome the effects of persecution?

Q.1x Have you experienced self-doubt due to the persecution? If so, describe it and tell how you have worked to overcome it:

_____
_____
_____

In the spaces below, please enter any additional notes on the chapter:

Lesson 2: How to Understand Divine Appointment

This chapter will help you understand what divine destiny is and how to recognize it.

Q2.a   How do you define what a "divine appointment" means?

_____

_____

_____

Q2.b   Read Habakkuk 2:3 NKJV, what does this verse mean to you?

_____

_____

_____

Q2.c   Do you understand the vision God has set for you?

_____

_____

_____

Q2.d   Describe your vision:

_____

_____

_____

Q2.e   Which of the following best describes how you are handling your God-given vision:

- o   I am fulfilling my vision
- o   I am still discovering my vision
- o   I have completed my vision
- o   Other, please describe:

_____

_____

_____

Encounters of a Divine Appointment

Q2.f   Describe an experience where you recognized God's divine appointment in a situation:

_____
_____
_____

Joshua, Moses is Dead

Q2.g   Read Joshua 1:1-3 KJV, how do these scriptures describe a divine appointment?

_____
_____
_____

Q2.h   What are the specific directions God gave Joshua?

_____
_____
_____

Q2.i   Do you recognize God's divine encounter with Joshua? Describe:

_____
_____
_____

Saul / Paul

Q2.j   Read Acts 9:3-6 NKJV, what did Jesus do to initiate a divine appointment with Saul?

_____
_____
_____

Q2.k   How did Saul respond to the divine appointment?

_____

_____

_____

Q2.l   What was the specific directive Jesus gave to Saul?

_____

_____

_____

Q2.m   Read Acts 9:11-12 NKJV, describe a time you were led by the Lord and you were unaware of where you were going:

_____

_____

_____

Q2.n   Read Psalm 32:8-9 in the NKJV, then read it again in The Passion Translation (TPT). Describe a time in your life when you knew you were being led by the Lord

_____

_____

_____

Q2.o   From the above scriptures, describe a time when you were stubborn and did not follow the Lord's leading in a situation:

_____

_____

_____

Paul wrote a prayer on how to receive spiritual wisdom in Ephesians 1:17-22, that is still relevant today. Pray this prayer for yourself every day to develop your spiritual wisdom and insight to the Word of God:

> *Heavenly father I ask you to grant me spiritual wisdom and revelation knowledge of Jesus, that my eyes of understanding will be opened and I am enlightened to know the hope of Your calling of what the riches of the glory of His inheritance are for me. I want to know and understand what is the exceeding greatness of your power toward me, who believe, according to the working of Your mighty power which works in Christ when God raised Him from the dead and seated Him at His right hand in the Heavenly places above the principality, powers, might and dominion and every name that is named, not only in this age but also in that which is to come. That everything that hinders me is put under Your feet for you gave him Jesus to be head over all things to the church In Jesus name Amen!*

In the spaces below, please enter any additional notes on the chapter:

Lesson 3: How Does God Guide Me?

My Guiding Journey

Q3.a Read Jeremiah 1:5 KJV, how can you relate to this scripture?

_____
_____
_____

Q3.b Read James 4:7 NKJV, describe an account when you applied this scripture to your life:

_____
_____
_____

Q3.c Describe a time in your life when you encountered a divine experience:

_____
_____
_____

Q3.d How did the divine encounter make you feel?

_____
_____
_____

Q3.e Reflect on the phrase, "Chase the Lord not as a perfect person, but as a person seeking perfection." List 3 ways you can seek perfection:

_____
_____
_____

God Guides by His Word

Q3.f   Read Proverbs 16:9 ESV, have you made plans for your life that the Lord has established? If so, describe:

_____

_____

_____

Q3.g   Have you made plans for your life you feel did not happen? If so, describe:

_____

_____

_____

Q3.h   Read Psalm 119:105 ESV, how has the Lord directed you in a specific way?

_____

_____

_____

Q3.i   Read Proverbs 6:23 ESV, List three ways you can apply this scripture for each point below:

- Commandment is a Lamp:

_____

_____

- Teaching is a light:

_____

_____

- Reproofs and discipline are a way of life:

_____

_____

Q3.j Read Isaiah 58:11 NLT, when you are feeling down, how can this scripture encourage you?

_____

_____

_____

Q3.k Read John 14:26 and John 16:13 NIV,

Who is the advocator? _____

What will the advocator do for you? _____

What is another name for Holy Spirit? _____

Where does the Holy Spirit's message come from? _____

Q3.l Read Proverbs 11:14 and Proverbs 1:5 NIV How can you use these scriptures as a basis of guidance?

_____

_____

_____

Q3.m How do you define discernment in your own words?

_____

_____

_____

Q3.n Read 1 Corinthians 12:4-11 NKJV, List any of the spiritual gifts you have and operate in:

_____

_____

_____

In the spaces below, please enter any additional notes on the chapter:

Lesson 4: How Do I Follow the Voice of God?

In this chapter, you will discover how to follow the voice of God and how to recognize God's voice and distinguish from other voices.

Q4.a Do you feel you currently recognize the voice of God?

___

Q4.b In the book, the example of a baby's growth stages depicts them learning to distinguish their mother's voice from their aunts' voice. What was the primary way the baby learned to recognize their mother's voice?

___

Q4.c What is the best way(s) for you to hear the voice of God more clearly?

___

An Example of Hearing God Through His Word

Q4.d Read Ephesians 4:31-32 NKJV, what are the instructions given in these verses?

___

Q4.e   How can you apply Ephesians 4:31-32 to your life?

_____

_____

_____

Q4.f   Read Matthew 18:21-22 NKJV, how would you respond if the Lord spoke these scriptures directly to you?

- ☐   I will readily obey
- ☐   I will act as if I did not hear it
- ☐   Other ways you can respond:

_____

_____

Q4.g   Read Colossians 3:16 NKJV, what is your responsibility for applying this scripture to your life?

_____

_____

_____

Q4.h   Read John 10:27 KJV, how do each of the points below represent how you can know, hear and follow the voice of God

- My sheep: _____

  _____

- Hear My voice: _____

  _____

- I know them: _____

  _____

- They follow Me: _____

  _____

Q4.i   Describe what these signs are telling you:

- Stop: _____
  _____

- Wait: _____
  _____

- Go: _____
  _____

Q4.j   Read Psalm 119:15-16 NKJ. If scriptures are the primary way the Lord speaks, then how does this scripture encourage you to hear God's voice?

_____
_____
_____

You Must Understand God's Voice

Q4.k   Read Psalm 119:27 NKJV, describe how you can apply this scripture to your life:

_____
_____
_____

Q4.l   Read Matthew 7:7-8 NKJV. Review the list of practical steps to hear God's voice listed in the book. Describe how you can use any of the steps in learning to hear God's voice.

_____
_____
_____

Q4.m   Read Psalm 3:5-6 NKJV, how can you apply these scriptures to hearing and following the voice of God?

_____
_____
_____

In the spaces below, please enter any additional notes on the chapter:

Lesson 5: Arriving in Destiny!

Everyone has a destiny! In this chapter you will learn how arriving in your destiny is not a piece of cake. You must do the work needed to enter your destiny.

Q5.a   Have you discovered your destiny? If so, describe it at a high level.

_____
_____
_____

Q5.b   What stage of your destiny are you in?

- ☐ Healing from a past relationship
- ☐ Sorting through the aftermath of divorce
- ☐ Getting past the loss of a loved one
- ☐ Coming from under persecution
- ☐ Thriving in your destiny
- ☐ Other, explain:

On the Road to Destiny!

Q5.c   Read James 1:2-4 TPT. What is the primary difficulty described that you could face?

_____
_____
_____

Q5.d   In James 1:2-4 TPT, what is your expected response?

_____
_____
_____

Q5.e   In James 1:2 TPT, it indicates that you will see difficulties as an opportunity, describe how you expected joy in a difficult situation:

_____

_____

_____

Q5.f   Read Hebrews 13:2 NLT, describe a time when a stranger came to your aid from out of nowhere:

_____

_____

_____

Q5.g   Read Psalm 23:4 TPT, list at least three promises from this scripture that are applicable to you:

_____

_____

_____

Q5.h   How has the Lord helped you through your darkest days?

_____

_____

_____

You Have Arrived at Destiny!

Q5.i   Now that you are in your destiny, how do you do what you believe that you are destined to do?

_____

_____

_____

Q5.j Do you feel equipped to do what you feel you were called to do?

_____
_____
_____

Q5.k Read John 10:10 TPT, what is the plan the devil has for you?

_____
_____
_____

Q5.l In the book, the following is a short list of common things you can do to ensure you stay on the road to your destiny:

- Know who you are
- Know why you were born
- Understand your purpose
- Discover your talents, strengths, and gifts
- Stay tapped into what you are truly passionate about

List three additional things you can do to stay on the road to your destiny:

_____
_____
_____

In the spaces below, please enter any additional notes on the chapter:

Lesson 6: How to Stay on Destiny's Track

In this lesson you will learn some different ways to stay on destiny's track without falling back to a previous state. This section will help you to identity your "good place". Whether that good place is recognizing your assignment from God, starting a new business, or getting over the past. You will feel a sense of relief and accomplishment knowing your destiny.

Q6.a John 10:10 TPT says, "…But I have come to give you everything in abundance, more than you expect – life in its fulness until you overflow." What are the promises to you in this scripture?

_____

_____

_____

Q6.b Other than the four points listed in the book to keep you moving forward, what are some other ways that can help you to continue moving forward?

_____

_____

_____

How Does Prayer Keep You on Track?

Q6.c List the main thing in your past that has the tendency to call you back to your past?

_____

_____

_____

Q6.d Read Romans 12:1-2 TPT. List the actional responses you should have in these scriptures:

_____

_____

_____

Q6.e   What do you believe will happen when you pray Romans 12:1-2?

_____
_____
_____

Q6.f   Read Philippians 4:6-7. How can these scriptures guard against your past?

_____
_____
_____

Q6.g   What is your current process to deal with anxiety? What can you do differently?

_____
_____
_____

Q6.h   List at least three techniques that you use to bring yourself back into peace of mind:

_____
_____
_____

Q6.i   Read Psalm 46:1; 10a NIV. What provisions are given to you?

_____
_____
_____

Q6.j   Read Philippians 2:5 KJV. How do you let your mind be "Christ-like"?

_____
_____
_____

Q6.k Read 2 Corinthians 10:3-5 TPT. These scriptures describe the spiritual warfare often experienced that keeps one from achieving their destiny. What can you do to defeat this type of spiritual attack?

Q6.l List at least three thoughts the enemy has used against you to keep you from moving forward:

How Does Wise Council Keep You on Track?

Q6.m In your own words, define "wisdom":

Q6.n Read James 1:5 TPT. According to this scripture, where do you get wisdom?

Q6.o Describe a time where you asked God for wisdom in a situation and He gave you the answer you were seeking:

Q6.p   Read Proverbs 19:20 AMP. What do you think about God's instructions to "Listen to wise council" and "accept correction"?

_____
_____
_____

Q6.q   Read Isaiah 11:2 NIV. List the characteristics of a wise council according to this scripture:

_____
_____
_____

How Do Strategic Plans Keep You on Track?

Q6.r   Read Jeremiah 29:11 NIV. A plan is a method or schema for doing, acting, or proceeding to something. What are the four things God is speaking of in this scripture?

_____
_____
_____

Q6.s   How important is it for you to have a strategic plan for your assignment? Please explain:

_____
_____
_____

Q6.t   Have you written a strategic Plan for the assignment God gave you? If not, why?

_____
_____
_____

Q6.u Describe a time when the phrase "Even when you cannot see God moving, He has already moved in your favor." was true for you:

_____

_____

_____

Q6.v Read Habakkuk 2:2 NKJV. What actions are you responsible for in this scripture?

_____

_____

_____

Q6.w Explain why it is important for you to write your vision and make it clear?

_____

_____

_____

How Does Perseverance Keep You on Track?

Q6.x Read Isaiah 43:18-19 NKJV. Why do these scriptures instruct you to NOT remember the former things? What should you expect God to do for you?

_____

_____

_____

Q6.y Read Luke 23:34 TPT and Matthew 6:15. How have you shown perseverance through forgiveness towards someone that has persecuted you in the past?

_____

_____

_____

Q6.z   Read Hebrews 10:33-37 NIV. Why do you need to persevere? What is in in for you?

_____

_____

_____

In the spaces below, please enter any additional notes on the chapter:

Lesson 7: Healing in the Emotions

In this lesson you will discover how to ensure you can receive healing in your emotions. Emotional healing does not mean you have a mental problem, it is just that some pressures can be too overwhelming to handle. In this section you will see how God is concerned about your emotional healing and that He has the answer to bring you back into emotional balance.

Q7.a   What is your understanding of emotional healing?

_____

_____

_____

Q7.b   In your own words, define "Emotions":

_____

_____

_____

Q7.c   Since emotions deal with a physiological experience that can affect the mind and cause an adverse reaction to a situation; do you recall a time when your emotions went "out of control?

_____

_____

_____

Q7.d   Extreme emotion is sometimes categorized as emotional illness. What are some characteristics that depict emotional illness?

_____

_____

_____

Q7.e   Have you ever experienced any of these characteristics, if so, which one(s)?

_____

_____

_____

Q7.f   Describe a time when you have witnessed an emotional outburst from a family member or a friend:

_____

_____

_____

Your Emotions Can Be Healed!

Q7.g   Describe your thoughts or beliefs about emotional healing:

_____

_____

_____

Q7.h   What are the four ways listed in the book that describe how you can "come to grips" with your emotional state of mind?

_____

_____

_____

Q7.i   Read Ephesians 6:10-13 KJV. In these scriptures, what is the believer fighting against? How do you defend against it?

_____

_____

_____

Q7.j Read 1 Peter 5:10 ESV. What are the promises you, the believer, are to expect after suffering?

_____

_____

_____

Q7.k Read Psalm 34:19 KJV and again in NIV. It is stated that the righteous will endure many afflictions or troubles. List three afflictions/troubles you are dealing with or have dealt with in the past:

_____

_____

_____

God's Plan for Healing You

Q7.l Read Job 42:10-17 NKJV. What did Job do that caused the Lord to restore all he had lost?

_____

_____

_____

Q7.m Read Jeremiah 29:11 ESV. Do you know the plan God has for you in your present season? If so, describe at a high level:

_____

_____

_____

Q7.n Do you feel you can accomplish what the Lord has given you to do?

_____

_____

_____

Q7.o Read 3 John 1:2 NKJV. In this simple prayer, what are the requests made for the believer?

What will it Take? FAITH?

Q7.p Read Mark 11:22-24 NKJV. In these scriptures, what do you have to do to exercise your faith?

Q7.q Read Matthew 15:28 TPT. Describe the attitude of the woman in this scripture:

Q7.r Without that attitude, what do you think the outcome would have been?

Q7.s Read Hebrews 11:1 in NKJV, TPT and AMP. What are the various descriptions of faith from each version?

Q7.t   How do you activate your faith?

_____

_____

_____

Q7.u   Read 2 Corinthians 5:7 NKJV. Describe how you walk by faith:

_____

_____

_____

Q7.v   Read Hebrews 11:6 TPT. What will it take to please God?

_____

_____

_____

In the spaces below, please enter any additional notes on the chapter:

Your One Page Strategic Plan

In the section below, write your high-level strategic plan for your God-given assignment:

Assignment Name:
GOALS:
Long term goals:
1.
2.
3
Short term goals:
1.
2.
3.
Success Measurements:
1.
2.
3.
STRATEGY:
Resource Assessment: people, infrastructure, finances etc. required to realize goals:
Implementation Plan: what will be done to meet deadlines?
Progress Assessment Plan: how will progress be monitored for success and revisions to implementation plan?
Timeline to completion
Start Date: Completion Date:
Initiation:
Planning:
Execution:
Monitoring and Controlling:
Closure:

In the spaces below, add any additional planning notes that will help you to get started, continue, or complete your assignment:

Conclusion

CONGRATULATIONS on completing this study guide! You have obtained various tools to assist you in moving forward in your God-given assignment.

As you embark on the next chapter in your life, I pray you will continue to grow in your relationship with God. Allow the Holy Spirit to lead you, guide you and most of all develop the person of Christ within you.

Going forward you can recognize when you have a divine encounter with God in a situation. You will no longer be resistant to the leading of the Holy Spirit, but you will willingly follow. You can feel comfortable with writing your vision and executing the plan as written. You can now get on track and stay on track to your destiny. Any emotional imbalances you know can be healed through the application of Godly council and the Word of God.

Lastly, if this study guide has been a blessing and a help to you, please share it with others. This guide is perfect for individual or group studies. Our challenge to you is that you take initiative to lead others into a deeper relationship with God by hosting a small group using the MOVE book and the MOVE Study Guide.

If you or your church or ministry is interested in leading a group of 15 or more, we have incentives to assist with bulk orders of the book and the study guide. Contact TaylorMade Publishing via email: info@taylormadepublishingfl.com or call (904) 323-1334. Visit our website for additional information: www.taylormadepublishingfl.com.

About the Author

𝔉𝔯𝔦𝔷𝔢𝔩𝔩𝔞 𝔇𝔬𝔫𝔢𝔤𝔞𝔫 𝔗𝔞𝔶𝔩𝔬𝔯 is a wife, mother, grandmother, Author, and Conference Speaker. She is an experienced Bible instructor with over 30 years of teaching experience.

Frizella's writing career began over 20 years ago. She has written and published four books to date. She has also composed and written a prayer journal and several ministry tracks. Her Christian background has provided her with a wealth of leadership experiences (i.e. children's ministry, youth ministry, women's ministry, prayer, and intercessory ministry as well as Pastoral) to glean from and share. You may find videos and Blogs on her website (www.frizelladonegantaylor.com) written to uplift and encourage.

Frizella's formal education includes a master's degree in Information Technology, Bachelor of Science in Management and Business, and an associate degree in Computer Programming.

Frizella along with her husband, Steve are Co-Owners of TaylorMade Publishing of Florida providing services to authors in the areas of coaching, proofreading, editing, formatting of eBook, book publishing and more. Learn more about TaylorMade Publishing at www.TaylorMadePublishingFL.com.

About the Publisher

TaylorMade Publishing was created by Steve and Frizella Taylor, a husband and wife team. It was birthed from a desire to publish their books without surrendering their rights and royalties to the traditional publishing companies. As authors who desire to publish and market their books, TaylorMade Publishing provides the resources to publish without the traditional hassles.

TaylorMade Publishing has developed a successful formula that allows new or established authors to choose services needed to get their books to market in the most efficient and economical way possible.

Our staff is committed to providing authors with an exceptional publishing experience, allowing them to focus their time and energy on their passion without the distractions, headaches and roadblocks often encountered in the publishing process.

TaylorMade Publishing

Books by Frizella

Changes, Changes, Changes:

God changes you into the image of Jesus by His Word

This book offers insight to a personal change in your Christian walk that helps your transformation to blossom into a beautiful butterfly. If you are ready to change your life, then this book will offer insights on how God wants to transform you into a new person to be used in His Kingdom.

Growing in the Lord sometimes bring challenges in our personal relationships. Here you will find some key points in dealing with these sensitive challenges. These key points will assist you with your personal growth in the Lord and help you discern relationships in your life.

- Understanding and receiving salvation
- Understanding and learning WHO Christ is
- Understanding and learning that your life can and will be transformed
- And much more

Author: Frizella Donegan

ISBN: 978-0-9968123-0-6

A Family That PRAYS

A Book of Prayers

Author: Frizella Donegan

ISBN: 978-0-9968123-2-0

The Bible teaches us that the effectual fervent prayer of the righteous avails much. However, what if one does not know how to pray or where to start? Where does that leave you? The disciples asked Jesus to teach them how to pray and today the Lord still teaches us how to pray and uses people to assist in that teaching.

In this book, you will find self-help prayers that will enable you to have a successful prayer life right away. You will learn how to pray effectively and get results. With a full understanding of what prayer is, it puts you on the right path of communicating with God. God is not moved by your tears, emotions, or begging. God is moved by His Word...His Promises in His Word. Therefore, you are to pray His word back to Him.

Noon Break Into HIS Presence

30-Day Devotional

In Psalms 55, King David utters some profound words that deal with trusting in God. When you must deal with treacherous people especially in the workplace, sometimes you need a midday break through!

This devotional has 30 exhortations that help keep in you in perfect peace because your mind will stay on the Lord Jesus! Psalm 55:17 confirms that noonday devotion is well within order. It simply says "Evening, and morning, and at noon, will I pray, and cry aloud: and he shall hear my voice." For the next 30 days, you will have a quick word at your fingertips within this devotional. Then you can start over again as the Word take root in your heart and more revelation is given to you from the Lord.

Author: Frizella Taylor

ISBN: 978-0-9968123-3-7

MOVE:

From Despondency to Destiny, Your Destiny Awaits

When you find yourself in a place where you do not hear the voice of God, do not see His hand moving in your life; you realize life has dealt you a raw hand in your marriage and it lead to divorce. A raw hand in your personal relationships with family, friends, co-workers, church folks and they all seem to be unbalanced and challenged. You may have experienced the death of a loved one or you are trying to work through personal persecutions.

Regardless of what issue you are experiencing, you may be feeling alone or stuck in your and unable to move forward. You must identify where you are and what is holding you back and why it is holding you back. We all have a destiny and it will include various divine appointments in your life's journeys.

This book will help you to identify which issues you may be facing. It will assist you in understanding what a divine appointment is and how it can catapult you in the right direction. That it is time for the Lord to lead you to the rock that is higher than you. The Bible reminds us in Psalm 61:3b; that the Lord is our strong tower from the enemy. While the enemy's plans are for you to miss your destiny by way of disrupting your divine appointment; please understand the Bible says the steps of the righteous are ordained of the Lord according to Psalm 37:23.

Therefore, when the enemy tries you, he may even send you off in another direction, remember, God's word is the true and that you are established by Him; in Him, through Him, and He directs you back to Himself. Be encouraged, do not give up and do not give in. The Lord is on your side and He has your back. I decree you will not miss your divine appointment, divine assignment, or divine destiny in Jesus name!!

Author: Frizella Taylor

ISBN: 978-0-9968123-4-4

www.ingramcontent.com/pod-product-compliance
Lightning Source LLC
Chambersburg PA
CBHW060501010526
44118CB00018B/2499